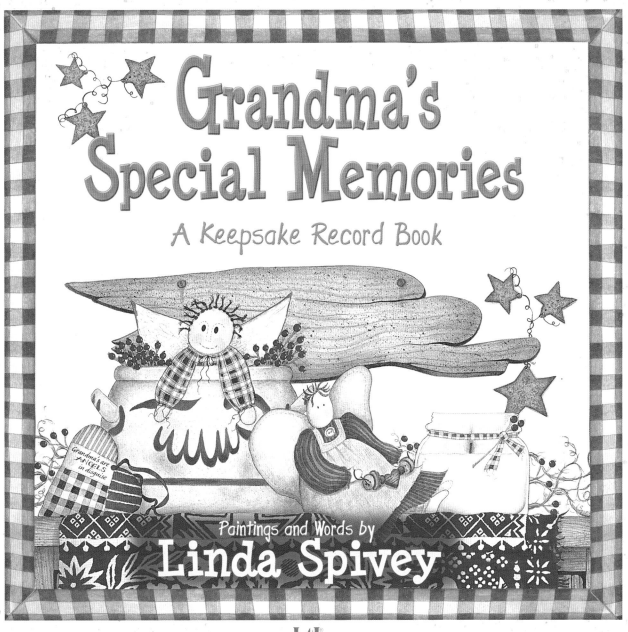

Grandma's Special Memories

A Keepsake Record Book

Paintings and Words by

Linda Spivey

HARVEST HOUSE PUBLISHERS

EUGENE, OREGON

Grandma's Special Memories

ISBN 0-7369-1471-4

Tell me about you, Grandma _____

With Love,

_____

*Happy times and bygone days are never lost…
In truth, they grow more wonderful
within the heart that keeps them.*
Kay Andrew

Grandma, the day you were born the angels must have been singing! Tell me about when and where you were born.

Grandma's are ANGELS in disguise

NEWCASTLE

Grandma, what is your full name? Do you know why you were given this name? Were you almost named something else?

_____

_____

What events were happening in the world when you were a little girl?

_____

_____

_____

Where did you live as a little girl? What are your favorite memories?

_____

_____

_____

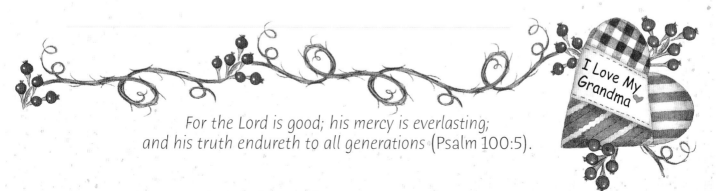

For the Lord is good; his mercy is everlasting;
and his truth endureth to all generations (Psalm 100:5).

Tell me, Grandma, about your mother. What is her full name? Her maiden name? When and where was she born? Where did she grow up?

What was your mother's educational background?

_____

_____

_____

Did your mother work a job? Tell me about it.

_____

_____

_____

What did your mother enjoy doing the most?

_____

_____

_____

Tell me about your father. What is his full name? When and where was he born? Where did he grow up?

What was his educational background? What did he do to earn a living?

What did he enjoy doing the most?

Photographs of You and Your Parents

The works of the Lord are great, sought out of all them that have pleasure therein. His work is honorable and glorious: and his righteousness endureth for ever (Psalm 111:2-3).

Grandma, I'd like to know about your grandparents. What are their full names? Where and when were they born? What are your favorite memories of them?

Your mother's mother:

_____

_____

Your mother's father:

_____

_____

Your father's mother:

_____

_____

Your father's father:

_____

_____

Grandma, tell me about your brothers and sisters. What are their names and birthdates?

Who did you have the most fun with growing up? What did you do together?

Tell me, Grandma, about your home and neighborhood when you were little. What are your fondest memories?

What was your bedroom like? Did you share it with anyone?

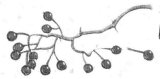

Behold, how good and how pleasant it is for brethren to live together in unity! It is like precious oil upon the head (Psalm 133:1-2).

Photographs of
You and Your Family

Photographs of
You and Your Family

God Bless Our Home

Grandma, tell me about the faith in your family as you were growing up.

Who gave you your first Bible, and how old were you?

What church did you go to as a youth, and what were your favorite activities?

What were your favorite religious traditions in your family and where did they originate from?

If you were baptized, tell me about it. How old were you? What family and friends shared this with you?

Grandma, did you have a special quilt or blanket? Was it handmade?

Every good gift and every perfect gift is from above, and cometh down from the Father of light (James 1:17).

Grandma, did you ever make a gift for anyone? What were some of the things you liked to make?

_____

_____

_____

_____

_____

Did you learn to sew or knit? Who taught you these skills? What are the things you like to make?

_____

_____

_____

_____

_____

Did you ever enter anything at the County Fair?

_____

_____

_____

What are your favorite springtime memories? Did you ever go fly a kite?

What memories, Grandma, do you have of Easter? Did you go to a sunrise service at church?

Did you get a special outfit to wear Easter morning?

What were your family's Easter traditions? Did you have Easter baskets and decorated eggs?

How have your traditions changed since you were a young girl?

Grandma, did you have a favorite doll or teddy bear? Who gave it to you? What did you name it?

A merry heart maketh a cheerful countenance (Proverbs 15:13).

What became of your favorite doll or teddy?

Did you have any other favorite toys?

Did you have any favorite board games? Who did you usually play these with?

When school was almost out for the summer, Grandma, what did you dream most about doing?

Think happy thoughts, O friend, in sunny weather!
Let gladness and thy spirit, hand in hand,
Wander across the daisied fields together.
Charles Poole Cleaves

Grandma, when summertime came, how did you keep cool?

What were your favorite activities? Did you have a bicycle? Tell me about it. Where would you ride?

Did your family go on vacations? Where have you gone, and what did you do?

Grandma, did you have a favorite pet while growing up? What made them so special?

Do you have a funny story about your pet?

Did you ever go camping? Were you ever a Girl Scout or a Campfire Girl?

Do you have any treehouse stories to tell me?

And whatsoever ye do,
do it heartily,
as to the Lord
(Colossians 3:23).

Grandma, when you were a young girl, what did you do to help in the kitchen?

_____

_____

_____

How old were you when you learned how to cook? What were the things you learned to make first?

_____

_____

_____

Was your mother a very good cook? Or your father? What kind of foods did they make most of the time?

_____

_____

_____

Favorite Family

Recipes

Apply thine heart unto instruction, and thine ears
to the words of knowledge
(Proverbs 23:12).

I have taught thee in the way of wisdom; I have
led thee in right paths
(Proverbs 4:11).

Wisdom is the principal thing; therefore get wisdom:
and with all thy getting get understanding
(Proverbs 4:7).

Show me thy ways, O Lord; teach me thy paths
(Psalm 25:4).

Grandma, tell me about your school days. What schools did you attend?

What was your favorite subject?

What was your least favorite subject?

Did you have a special teacher? How did he or she influence you?

Tell me more about your elementary school days, Grandma. What did you do at recess?

_____

_____

_____

_____

What activities did you participate in?

_____

_____

_____

Did you go on any school trips?

_____

_____

_____

_____

Tell me about your high school days. What school did you go to? What year did you graduate? How many were in your graduating class? Tell me about your graduation day.

Did you go to your school prom? Who did you go with? Tell me about this special day.

School Pictures

School Pictures

Grandma, tell me about the best thing you ever did with a friend.

*A friend loveth
at all times,
and a brother
is born for
adversity
(Proverbs 17:17).*

Tell me about your best friends when you were a young girl. What were the things you liked to do together?

Who were your best friends in high school? What did you do together?

Do you still keep in contact with any of your old friends?

Photographs of Friends

Photographs of Friends

Tell me, Grandma, what you love about autumn.

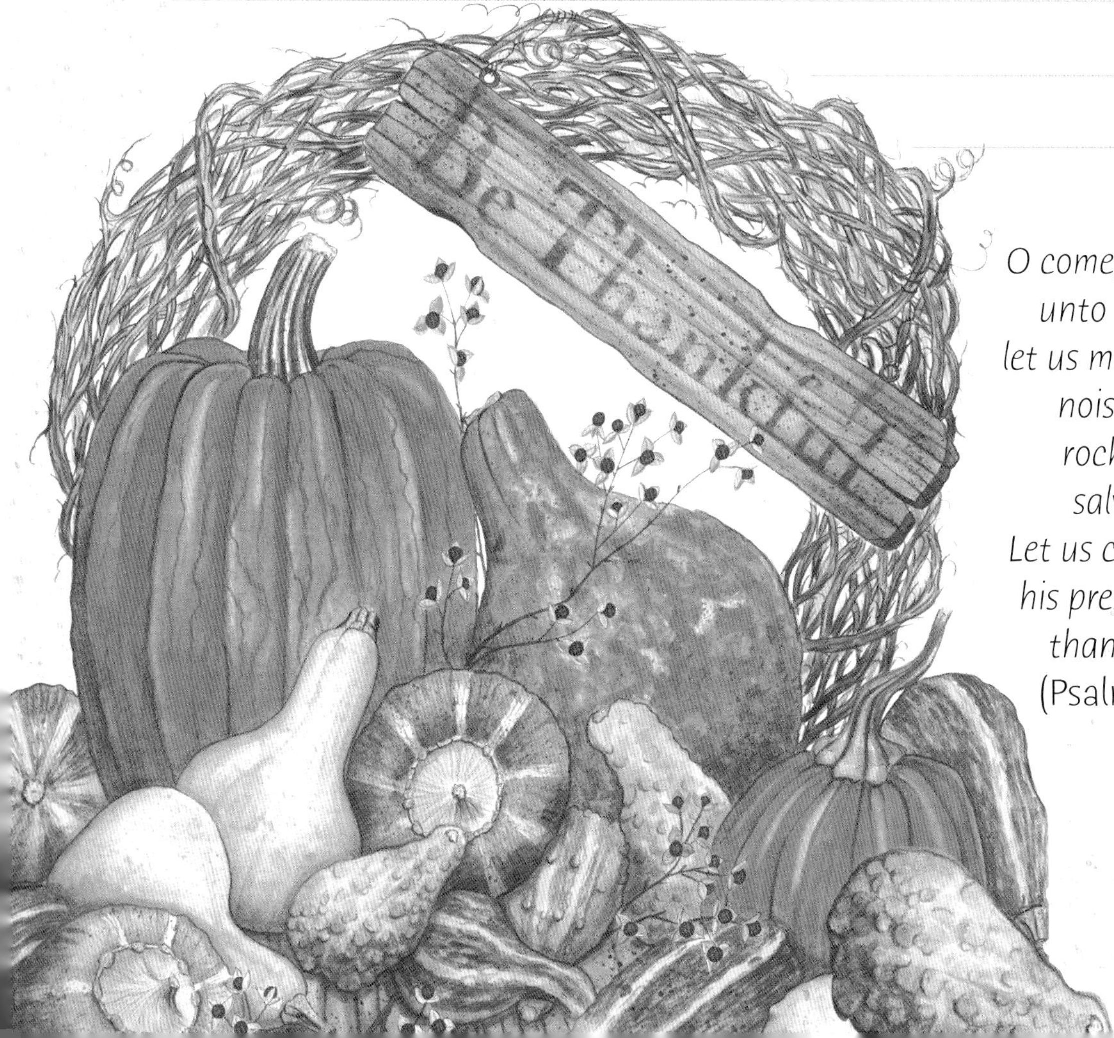

O come, let us sing
unto the Lord:
let us make a joyful
noise to the
rock of our
salvation.
Let us come before
his presence with
thanksgiving
(Psalm 95:1-2).

Grandma, how did your family celebrate
Thanksgiving? Who would say the blessing?

What made this day special to you?

What special foods were served? Who did all the cooking?

Grandma, tell me your fondest memories of Christmas when you were young.

Tell me about the Christmas traditions in your family. Did you hang up a Christmas stocking?

What religious traditions were part of your family celebrations?

What was the most memorable gift you received when you were a young girl? Who gave it to you? Did someone ever make you a special gift?

And the angel said unto them, Fear not: for, behold, I bring you good tidings of great joy, which shall be to all people
(Luke 2:10).

Christmas Photographs

Christmas Photographs

Grandma, what would you like me to know most about you?

_____

_____

_____

What are your hopes and dreams for me, Grandma?

_____

_____

_____

So if you have a grandma,
Thank the good Lord up above,
And give grandma hugs and kisses,
For grandmothers are to love.
Lois Wyse